Book of Remembrance

Stephen E. Canup

WISDOM NUGGETS FROM THE BACK OF MY BIBLES

Do you want to learn more about being a disciple of Jesus Christ?

A "DISCIPLE" IS A "DISCIPLINED LEARNER".

Which three topics interest you?

These are not Bible Correspondence Courses where you send lessons back; you simply need to be willing to study them, learn something new, and share them with others.

Choose only three topics. Send us a letter with the topic numbers and names you want us to mail to you.

After selecting *no more than three* teachings, send your request to:

Freedom in Jesus Prison Ministries
Attn: Teachings
P.O. Box 939
Levelland, TX 79336

Be sure to plainly print your full name, I.D. Number, full name of facility, and your complete mailing address.

1. Biblical Fasting
2. Disciples of Christ
3. God's Love for You
4. The Gospel of Jesus Christ
5. True Remnant Believers Choose Wisely
6. Judgment is Coming
7. The Last Days
8. Do Not Be Deceived
9. Do Not Fear
10. Hell
11. The Fear of the Lord
12. Discerning God's Voice
13. Dealing with Temptation
14. Sanctification and Holiness
15. Do You Know Jesus? Does Jesus "Know" You?
16. Forgiveness
17. Jesus is Coming Again
18. Holy Spirit Empowerment
19. Jesus is the Only Way
20. Repentance
21. The Rapture and the Last Days
22. Effective Prayer
23. Pattern and Purpose of Prayer
24. Faith
25. Spiritual Warfare - Part 1
26. Spiritual Warfare - Part 2
27. Spiritual Warfare - Part 3
28. Heaven
29. Praise and Worship

Book of Remembrance

Book of Remembrance

*Wisdom Nuggets from
the Back of my Bibles*

Stephen E. Canup

Special thanks to Rev. Don Castleberry,
Founder, Freedom in Jesus Prison Ministries

Published by:
Freedom in Jesus Prison Ministries
www.fijm.org | info@fijm.org

Acknowledgements

EVERYONE NEEDS A MATURE SPIRITUAL MENTOR and trusted accountability partner. I love and appreciate Don Castleberry for fulfilling this role for me. His trust, time and commitment to me have been invaluable. He has become one of my very best friends.

Rev. Don Castleberry is the Founder of Freedom in Jesus Prison Ministries. Learn more about this anointed prison ministry at *www.fijm.org* or, write to Freedom in Jesus Prison Ministries, P.O. Box 939, Levelland, TX 79336. You may e-mail us at *info@fijm.org*

Special thanks to Kevin Williamson for cover creation, layout and design assistance. For inquiries about his work, contact Kevin at *kevin@kevinwilliamsondesign.com*

Appreciation is also expressed for printing and shipping services through Perfection Press. For information contact Robert Riggs, *rriggs@printedtoperfection.com*

Copyright 2024© by Stephen Canup. All rights reserved.

All Scripture quotations, unless otherwise indicated, are taken from the Holy Bible, New International Version®, NIV®. Copyright ©1973, 1978, 1984, 2011 by Biblica, Inc.™ Used by permission of Zondervan. All rights reserved worldwide. www.zondervan.comThe "NIV" and "New International Version" are trademarks registered in the United States Patent and Trademark Office by Biblica, Inc.™

Scripture taken from the Amplified Bible (AMPCE), Copyright © 1954, 1958, 1962, 1964, 1965, 1987 by The Lockman Foundation. Used by permission.

Table of Contents

Dedication ix

Introduction xi

Encouragement 1

Abundant Life 11

The Word of God 49

Discipleship and Witnessing 65

Prayer and Devotion 113

Salvation 133

You Can Have "The Real Thing" 163

You Can Receive the Baptism
in the Holy Spirit 167

Dedication

THIS BOOK IS DEDICATED in loving memory of my father, Wayne M. Canup, who graduated to Heaven in 1981 at the too young age of 58. He was a wonderful dad, a dedicated husband, and a committed Christian. A Deacon in the Baptist Church, Wayne was an active participant and supporter of his Pastors and the local church. Most of all, he was a lover and follower of Jesus Christ.

My dad was the eternal optimist and loved to listen to and read positive, motivating books and articles. He was diligent to make notes, highlight paragraphs, record quotations, and share books-all with the motivation to inspire and encourage himself and others. His motivational gifts were encouragement and leadership. I must have inherited his zeal and drive to encourage because I too like to inspire, encourage and teach others.

One of my fondest memories are the summer camping trips he took all of the family on to the mountains of northern New Mexico. My favorite place to be is still in mountainous regions, particularly in the summer. In fact, the mountain resort where I go to write in Red River, NM, is only an hour or so from where we used to camp. The cover art is specifically for the two of us.

I am forever indebted to my father, Wayne Canup. I loved and respected him. I look forward to being re-united with him in Heaven.

Introduction

When I gave my heart to Jesus in 2009 in prison at age 57, I totally surrendered the rest of my life to serving Him. I found so much hope in receiving His finished work at the Cross, that a passionate fire of purpose was ignited in me to share the Good News with anyone who would listen. If God could change me, and He did, I wanted everyone to know He can change them and give them hope too. If He can use me, none of us are too damaged or too far gone to be utilized in His Kingdom work.

My study of God's Word awakened the desire to encourage and teach others. As a result, it is natural for me to write down quotations, and short paragraphs that inspire, teach and encourage me. Certainly, these "keepsakes" are part of the spiritual warfare weapons arsenal that God has provided me so that I can equip others.

Over the years, my "go to" place to record the wisdom gems I find in my studies is in the back of my favorite Bibles. I share them here in this book with you in the hope they will bless you as they have blessed me.

I did not always note the source of the quotation, thought or teaching when I wrote them in my Bibles, but where I did I have given proper credit in the pages which follow. In no way have I ever intended to plagiarize others so I ask their forgiveness in advance for any unattributed quotations.

May God bless you abundantly in every way, every day, as you devote yourself to Him and His Word.

Encouragement

God Has a Plan for You

" For I know the plans I have for you," declares the Lord, "plans to prosper you and not to harm you, plans to give you hope and a future. Then you will call on me and come and pray to me, and I will listen to you. You will seek me and find me when you seek me with all your heart. I will be found by you," declares the Lord, "and will bring you back from captivity..."

Jehovah, *Jeremiah 29:11-14a*

Speak Courage

Speaking encouragement is to speak courage into someone's life!

Born to Win

"When we were born again, we were born to win."

Dr. Adrian Rogers, *Adrianisms, Volume 2*

God Opens Windows

When the world closes a door, God opens a window!

The Will of God

The will of God won't take you where the grace of God can't keep you!

Purpose

"Failure in the past does not nullify purpose in the future."

Dr. Adrian Rogers, *Adrianisms, Volume 2*

Healer and Restorer

God is the Healer of broken dreams and the Restorer of stolen years.

Trials and Trouble

God is not here to keep you from trouble; He's here to go through trouble with you.

He will Never Leave You

"No one will be able to stand against you all the days of your life. As I was with Moses, so I will be with you; I will never leave you nor forsake you."

Jehovah, *Joshua 1:5*

God is at Work

"Just because you cannot see God working, does not mean He is not at work."

Dr. Adrian Rogers, *Adrianisms, Volume 2*

The Waves

It is safer on the waves with Jesus than in the boat without Him.

God Still has a Plan

If you woke up this morning, and you are still here–God still has a plan for your life!

With Open Arms

No matter what is happening in your life, know that God is waiting for you with open arms.

When God Says No

"When God says 'no,' it's because He has something better in store for you."

Dr. Adrian Rogers, *Adrianisms, Volume 2*

Wings of an Eagle

God doesn't want to give you the wings of a dove to fly away; He wants to give you the wings of an eagle to soar over your problems right where you are.

His Child

You are not your work.

You are not your number.

You are not what you own.

You are a child of the King of kings and the Lord of lords.

Trust Him.

God is For You

"What, then, shall we say in response to these things? If God is for us, who can be against us?"

Paul the Apostle, *Romans 8:31*

Jesus Gives Life

"The thief comes only to steal and kill and destroy; I have come that they may have life, and have it to the full."

Jesus, *John 10:10*

Abundant Life

Abundant Life

Jesus came to give us abundant life. (John 10:10b).

God gives us abundant mercy (Numbers 14:18).

God gives us abundant provision (2 Chron. 11:23).

God gives us abundant kindness (Nehemiah 9:17).

God gives us abundant pardon (Isaiah 55:7).

God gives us abundant peace (Psalm 37:11).

God gives us abundant grace (Romans 5:17).

Do Not Neglect Abundant Life

"It's a serious thing to neglect the abundant life God offers, as Moses warns in Deuteronomy 28:47-48: 'Because you did not serve the Lord your God with joy and gladness of heart, for the abundance of everything, therefore you shall serve your enemies, whom the Lord will send against you, in hunger, in thirst, in nakedness, and in need of everything; and He will put a yoke of iron on your neck until He has destroyed you.'"

Dr. David Jeremiah

Abundant, Overcoming Life

- Jesus came to give us abundant life (John 10:10).

- We are overcomers by faith, love and obedience (1 John 5:1-5).

- We are overcomers by Jesus' Blood and our testimony (Revelation 12:11).

- There are rewards for overcomers (Revelation 2:7, 11, 17, 26-28; Rev. 3:5, 12, 21).

- In Christ we are "more than conquerors", "super-victors" (Romans 8:35-39).

- In order to live the abundant life we must be transformed (Romans 12:2).

- "God does not give us overcoming life. He gives us life as we overcome."

    Hudson Taylor, Missionary to China

Character Matters

In the last days the Scriptures indicate people will call evil good and good evil. We live in a world where we are challenged daily to compromise our convictions and thereby undermine our destiny. The Word of God is clear, whatever we sow we will reap. In Jeremiah 29:11, we learn God has a future and hope for us, which is good news! But we have a responsibility to cooperate with God by making quality decisions.

Here are five simple things that we can do to help us continue on the path to positive destiny:

1. Watch your thoughts for they become your words.

2. Watch your words for they become your actions.

3. Watch you actions for they become your habits.

4. Watch your habits for they become your character.

5. Watch your character for it becomes your destiny.

6. See Philippians 4:8. Think on these things.

Provision

God will provide where He guides!

All You Need

Jesus is all you need. Unfortunately, sometimes you don't know it until Jesus is all you've got.

A Purpose to Die For

"Man has not truly lived until he has a purpose that he is willing to die for; he has only existed."

Don G. Castleberry, *Founder of Freedom in Jesus Prison Ministries*

Grace

"Grace is the multifaceted ability of God that flows to and through the lives of His humble children."

Pastor Jared Baker

Pay it Forward

"When we know we have been forgiven, we are empowered to forgive others. We want to give what we have received, to pay forward the grace that changed us."

Jim Denison

Contentment

Contentment is realizing that God has given you, in your present circumstances, everything you need to remain victorious in Christ.

God at the Center

How do you know when God is at the
center of your life?
When God is at the center, you worship.
When He's not, you worry.
Worry is the warning light that God has been
shoved to the sideline.

Emptiness

You never get so empty as when you are
filled up with yourself.

Life Abundantly

There is a difference between having life, and
having life more abundantly.

God's Plans

Just because God's actions don't fit our plans does not mean He does not have a plan for us.

Freedom

Freedom does not give us the right to do what we please, but to do what pleases God.

The Spirit of Life

"Therefore, there is now no condemnation for those who are in Christ Jesus, because through Christ Jesus the law of the Spirit who gives life has set you free from the law of sin and death."

Paul the Apostle, *Romans 8:1-2*

Humility

Acknowledging our total dependence on God and seeking His will for every decision. It is the displacement of self by the enthronement of God. Where God is all, self is nothing.

Gratefulness

Expressing sincere appreciation to God and others for the ways in which they have benefited our lives. It is the opposite of pride. People who are grateful realize that everything comes from the hand of God and is designed for their good.

Reverence

Humbling ourselves in the presence of a God-given authority and expressing honor with a gift (e.g. God – tithes; government – taxes; aged parents – financial assistance).

Truthfulness

Earning future trust by accurately reporting past facts.

Deference

Limiting my freedom in order to not cause others to be weakened or offended. It is also postponing words, attitudes or actions that would cause others to be offended.

Gentleness

Supporting others during their time of weakness so that they can achieve their full potential in the Lord.

Wisdom

Seeing and responding to life from God's point of view rather than from our own perspective. A wise person is a peacemaker; loves those who rebuke him; learns from his mistakes and the mistakes of others; controls his tongue; and, listens to counsel and instruction.

Faith

Recognizing God's will for a given situation and acting upon it.

Compassion

Responding to a deep need with a longing to do whatever is necessary to meet it. A compassionate person looks past the faults of others and sees the hurting person on the inside. He then acts to help heal those hurts.

Forgiveness

Responding to offenses in such a way that the power of God's love can work through us to heal our offenders.

Sincerity

Being as genuine on the inside as we appear to be on the outside.

Virtue

The power of a life that is in harmony with the holy standards of God.

Discernment

The ability to distinguish between good and evil in order to make wise decisions.

Persuasiveness

Guiding vital truths around the mental roadblocks of other people. Also, to guide another person's thoughts by a series of convincing statements.

Joyfulness

Consists of the bright spirit and radiant countenance that comes with being in full fellowship with the Lord.

Endurance

Experiencing the power of God's love by rejoicing in trials and tribulations. Also, not giving up and getting frustrated, upset or bitter.

Worrying

You can't change the past, but you will ruin the present by worrying about the future.

Glory

Praise, greatness or honor that people can see or sense, usually of God. Also, splendor, fame or magnificence.

Pain

"When all we see is our pain, it's then we lose sight of God."

William P. Young, *The Shack*

Don't Forget

"Don't forget in the darkness what you have learned in the light."

Don G. Castleberry, *Founder of Freedom in Jesus Prison Ministries*

Picture Jesus

"Why is it when we imagine our future (which is almost always dictated by fear or worry), rarely, if ever, do we picture Jesus there with us?"

William P. Young, *The Shack*

Imagined Fears

"It is impossible for us to take control over our future, because it isn't even real, nor will it ever be real. The person who lives by imagined fears will not find freedom in the love of Jesus. To the degree that we project these imagined fears into the future and give them a place in our lives, we neither believe Jesus is good, nor do we know deep in our hearts that He loves us."

William P. Young, *The Shack*

A Greater Reality

"This life is only the anteroom of a greater reality to come. No one reaches their full potential in this world. It's only preparation for what God has had in mind for us all along."

William P. Young, *The Shack*

Shadows

"The darkness hides the true size of fears and lies and regrets; the truth is they are more shadows than reality, so they seem bigger in the dark. When the light shines into the places where they live inside of you, you start to see them for what they are. Jesus is the Light."

William P. Young, *The Shack*

Above all Else

"Above all else, remember, God is especially fond of you!"

William P. Young, *The Shack*

New Ending

Though no-one can go back and make a brand new start, anyone can start from now and make a brand new ending.

In Reverse

"Faith means believing in advance what will only make sense in reverse."

Philip Yancey

Finished

You are not finished when you lose; you are finished when you quit.

A Fruitful Life

"The secret to a fruitful life is, in brief, to pour out to others and want nothing for yourself, and to leave yourself utterly in the hands of God and not care what happens to you."

The School of Christ Textbook, page 177

Choices

Once we make our choices, our choices make us!

Victory

"We don't fight for victory;

we fight from victory!"

Joseph Prince

Total Forgiveness

"Hopeful, satisfied living is not possible when overwhelming guilt is unresolved in the life of any person. In his own deep need, Robert Johnson found resolution of his own guilt through faith in Christ. Robert said, 'I am not living in tomorrow. I am not living in yesterday. I need Jesus today. I need His love and comfort today…We can trust Him and accept ourselves with the same love, knowing that we are forgiven, cleansed, healed in body and soul.'

"When he finally called on the Lord for mercy and deliverance God was there bringing pardon and peace. The greater miracle is that Robert Johnson was finally able to accept total forgiveness and forgive himself."

From: *Disciple in Prison, Robert A. Johnson,*
in the introduction by Chaplain Ray

The Spirit Gives Life

"But if Christ is in you, then even though your body is subject to death because of sin, the Spirit gives life because of righteousness. And if the Spirit of him who raised Jesus from the dead is living in you, he who raised Christ from the dead will also give life to your mortal bodies because of his Spirit who lives in you."

Paul the Apostle, *Romans 8:10-11*

Principles to Live By

Here are eight principles to live your life by:

1. I will do all things as unto the Lord (Romans 14:1-3, 5-8).
2. I will live in light of the judgment seat of Christ (Romans 14:10-11).
3. I will consider my weaker brother in all I do (Romans 14:13-21).
4. I will do nothing unless I'm sure it is right to do (Romans 14:22-23).
5. I will do all things to the glory of my God (1 Cor. 10:22-31; Psalm 19:1).
6. I will avoid what may appear wrong even if I know it's not (1 Thess. 5:21-22).
7. I will abstain from things which would enslave me (1 Cor. 6:12).
8. I will seek always to do what I believe Jesus would do (Rom. 12:1-2; 1 Pet. 2:21; Rom. 14:5b).

Look Up

Quit looking back; look up. Let God restore!

An Endless Hope

Man's way leads to a hopeless end – God's way leads to an endless hope.

Martin Luther's Last Words

In the final moment, his halting voice whispered the glorious message:

"Who... hath... my Word... shall... not... see... death."

Never Forget

"Never forget, how deep you go with God will determine how high you go in life."

Glenn Arekion

Grace

God can never love you more; He can never love you less. This is part of grace.

What the holiness of God demanded, the love of God provided. This is part of grace too!

Your End

"Your beginning does not have to determine your end!"

Joyce Meyer

God's Heart

"When we can't see God's Hand, we must trust His Heart."

Dr. Morris Sheets

A Little Faith

"A little faith will bring your soul to Heaven, but a lot of faith will bring Heaven to your soul."

Dwight L. Moody

The Past is Past

Don't let yesterday's failures
bankrupt tomorrow's efforts.
Let the past be past at last!
Forgive yourself and others.

Give

We make a living by what we get; we make a life by what we give.

His Presence

God's presence with us is one of His greatest presents to us.

Destiny

Destiny is not a matter of chance,

it is a matter of choice.

When Things Look Dark

"When things look darkest to the world, they

look brightest to the Christian. Our King is

coming back!"

Vance Havner

A World in Trouble

"The world is in trouble, but Jesus came to rescue

us from it's final consequences."

Dr. Erwin Lutzer

Endure

"If hope did not whisper in our ear that tomorrow will be better, how would anyone have the encourage to endure today?"

Robert Burns

What's In It for Me?

The answer to the question,

"What's in it for me?"

"What tremendous benefits will be yours – eternal life, forgiveness, peace, joy, love, fellowship, Jesus Christ as your Lord, God as your Father, the Holy Spirit as your life, a sure home in Heaven, and lasting security against all the forces of evil!"

Emmaus Correspondence Course

God's Love

"There is nothing the Christian can do to make God love him more, or love him less. God's love for His people is infinite and unconditional."

John Blanchard

God is Thinking about You

"God is thinking about you. God loves you. He would like to talk to you sometime. He's a lot more fun to be with you than you know."

Dr. Marvin Overton

The Truth of God

"When the child of God loves the Word of God and sees the Son of God, he is changed by the Spirit of God into the image of God for the glory of God because he has found the truth of God."

Dr. Adrian Rogers, *Adrianisms, Volume 2*

Joys Tomorrow

God allows sorrows and tears today to open our hearts to the joys of tomorrow.

The Love of God

"No matter who you are, you can never be completely fulfilled unless you allow the love of the living God to fill your life and your being, so that it can be reflected in your way of life."

Solly Ozrevech

Depression

Depression is the impression left by fear.

Sit Still

"When a train goes through a tunnel and it gets dark, you don't throw away the ticket and jump off. You sit still and trust the Engineer."

Corrie Ten Boom

Starting Over

"Remember this: failure isn't permanent unless you fail to get up. So pick yourself up, dust yourself off, and trust God. He will make it right. Warren Wiersbe had this advice, "No matter how badly we have failed, we can always get up and begin again. Our God is the God of new beginnings, and don't forget: the best time to begin again is now."

100 days of Prayer for a Righteous Man

Faith

Faith is not believing that God can do everything, but that He can and will do it for you.

Miracles

A miracle is a supernatural intervention into the natural problems and circumstances of life!

Sunshine

"When I met Christ, I felt that I had swallowed sunshine."

E. Stanley Jones

Never the Same

"No man is ever the same after God has laid His Hand upon him."

A.W. Tozer

Where You Can Be

"God not only sees where you are,

He sees where you can be!"

Joyce Meyer

All of Me

"True faith, in God's eyes, has nothing to do with the size or amount of work you aim to accomplish. Rather, it has to do with the focus and direction of your life. God is not as concerned with your grand vision as He is with who you are becoming. He is more interested in winning all of me than He is in my winning all the world for Him."

David Wilkerson

Free Will

God will not violate your free will, but He will love you into a decision!

Transformation

True transformation results when Christ and His Word renew our minds so that our vision, values and plans are governed by God's revelation and eternal truth, rather than by the world's temporal and deceptive pattern.

Future Potential

My present position is not an indication of my future potential in God!

Made for Another World

"If I find in myself a desire which no experience in this world can satisfy, the most probable explanation is that I was made for another world."

C.S. Lewis, *Made for Heaven*

Guilt and Shame

"Guilt says you did that; shame says you are that!"

Graham Cooke

Fuel for Faith

Humility opens us up to the grace of God which fuels our faith.

Opposition

"If there is no opposition, there is no victory."

Dr. Adrian Rogers, *Adrianisms,* **Volume 2**

Faith

"Faith is never blind, it sees and hears what God has said and what God has graced one with, and then it acts upon and opens up the gift of grace God has already given!"

Pastor Jared Baker

The Detour

The devil has not destroyed your life! Rather, you are simply on a detour on your way to the destiny God has designed for you!

In God's Hands

"I have held many things in my hands, and I have lost them all; but whatever I have placed in God's hands, that I still possess."

Martin Luther

Eternal Life

"Whoever believes in the Son has eternal life, but whoever rejects the Son will not see life, for God's wrath remains on them."

John the Baptist, *John 3:36*

The Word of God

The Word is Alive

"For the word of God is alive and active. Sharper than any double-edged sword, it penetrates even to dividing soul and spirit, joints and marrow; it judges the thoughts and attitudes of the heart. Nothing in all creation is hidden from God's sight. Everything is uncovered and laid bare before the eyes of him to whom we must give account."

Hebrew 4:12-13

Bible Study

The object of Bible study is not a full head, but a changed heart.
Of ultimate importance is not how well you have mastered the Bible, but how well it has mastered you!

The Oasis

Prison is a wilderness. God's Word is an oasis.

Transformation

"Be not conformed to the world but be transformed by the renewing of your mind..."

Romans 12:2

Transformation results when Christ and His Word renew our minds so that our vision, values and plans are governed by God's revelation and eternal truth, rather than by the world's temporal and deceptive pattern.

Sin

"The Bible is the only Book that gives us any indication of the true nature of sin, and where it came from."

Oswald Chambers

Timeless Questions

"There is one reason why the books of the Bible are just as relevant today as when they were written. The Bible deals with timeless questions. Who are we? Where did we come from? Why are we here? Where are we going? How should we live? Can you think of any questions more important than these? How can we ignore them?"

Billy Graham, *The Journey*

His Word is Truth

"I have given them your word and the world has hated them, for they are not of the world any more than I am of the world. My prayer is not that you take them out of the world but that you protect them from the evil one. They are not of the world, even as I am not of it. Sanctify them by the truth; your word is truth."

Jesus, *John 17:14-17*

Ignorance

"If you are ignorant of God's Word, you will always be ignorant of His will."

Billy Graham, *The Journey*

Knowing God's Will

Knowing God's will comes by seeking to be transformed by God's Word "inside out" and refusing to be shaped by the world "outside in".

See Romans 12:2

A Fool

In the Old Testament language of Psalms and Proverbs, a "fool" is an individual who makes choices as if God doesn't exist and lives as if God hasn't spoken.

Not a Burden

In 1 John 5:3, it says that the commands of God are not a burden, and so if the Word of God is sitting on you like a burden right now, it's because the Spirit of God is convicting you to make some changes in your life. I promise you that if you make that change, if you humble yourself before God and say, 'Yes, Lord', you'll see that burden quickly lifted. The heaviness of the Word is the wonderful conviction of the Spirit, that when acted upon becomes a joy. God's Word is our delight and in our obedience to it we find all the treasures and riches of Christ. I commend it to you now and for the rest of your life.

Understanding

"Don't worry about what you do not understand; worry about what you do understand in the Bible but do not live by."

Corrie Ten Boom

Be Thoroughly Equipped

"All Scripture is God-breathed and is useful for teaching, rebuking, correcting and training in righteousness, so that the servant of God may be thoroughly equipped for every good work."

Paul the Apostle, *2 Timothy 3:16-17*

Studying Scripture

When studying a verse you must observe, then interpret, then apply. Make detailed observations, ask interpretive questions, apply and interpret for your life.

Ask yourself the following. Is there a/an:

- Sin to forsake?
- Promise to claim?
- Example to follow?
- Command to obey?
- Stumbling block to avoid?

The acronym SPECS will help you remember.

Interpreting the Bible

When trying to interpret the Bible:

- Look at the overall purpose of the passage.

- See to whom the passage is addressed.

- Look at the context immediately before and after the verse you are studying.

- Try to determine more from the original language meanings.

- Interpret it literally – "When the plain sense of Scripture makes common sense, seek no other sense; therefore, take every word at its primary, ordinary, usual, literal meaning unless the facts of the immediate context studied in light of the related passages and axiomatic and fundamental truths, indicate clearly otherwise."

Dr. David Cooper

Bible Study Guidelines

Here are some guidelines for learning from the Bible:

- Begin with prayer.
- Read the Bible.
- Study the Bible.
- Meditate on the Bible.
- Read what others have written on the Bible.
- Obey the Bible.
- Pass it on to others.

God Keeps His Promises

"There are over 7,000 promises in His Word, and He keeps them all!"

Dr. Adrian Rogers, *Adrianisms, Volume 2*

The Fulfillment of the Law

"Do not think that I have come to abolish the Law or the Prophets; I have not come to abolish them but to fulfill them. For truly I tell you, until heaven and earth disappear, not the smallest letter, not the least stroke of a pen, will by any means disappear from the Law until everything is accomplished."

Jesus, *Matthew 5:17-18*

Knowing Christ

To know Christ, the Living Word, is to know and love the Bible, the written Word.

A Well-fed Soul

A well-read Bible is a sign of a well-fed soul!

Know, Stow, Show, Sow

The Bible: Know it in your head, stow it in your heart, show it in your life, sow it in the world!

Listen

God speaks through His Word to those who listen with their heart.

Knowing God

"How can we know the God of the Bible if we don't know the Bible of God?"

"Study the Bible to know about God. Obey the Bible to really know God."

Dr. Adrian Rogers, *Adrianisms, Volume 2*

God Comforts Us

"Scripture doesn't tell us that God wipes away our sadness in this life, but it does tell us that God is faithful and will comfort us."

Dave Brannon, *RBC Ministries*

Be Sure

The Blood makes us safe; the Book makes us sure.

A Child of God

"The Spirit of God with the Word of God makes a child of God!"

J. Vernon McGee

The Trinity

The Bible reveals that there is one eternal God, with one essence, existing in three persons who are equal yet distinct: God the Father and God the Son and God the Holy Spirit. All three are together in unity, equal and co-eternal. They are both one and three. They have one will. They always work together, and not even the smallest thing is done by one without the instant agreement of the other two. A.W. Tozer said, "The doctrine of the Trinity... is truth for the heart. The fact that it cannot be satisfactorily explained, instead of being against it, is in its favor. Such a truth had to be revealed; no one could have imagined it."

Scriptures evidencing the Trinity together: Isaiah 6:8; 61:1; Matthew 3:16-17; 28:19; Luke 1:35; John 14:16; 15:6; Acts 7:55; 10:38; Romans 1:4; 2 Corinthians 13:14; Ephesians 2:18; Hebrews 9:14; 1 Peter 1:2; 1 John 5:7.

God's Word Accomplishes His Purposes

"As the rain and the snow
come down from heaven,
and do not return to it
without watering the earth
and making it bud and flourish,
so that it yields seed for the sower and bread
for the eater,
so is my word that goes out from my mouth:
It will not return to me empty,

but will accomplish what I desire

and achieve the purpose for which I sent it."

Jehovah, *Isaiah 55:10-11*

Discipleship and Witnessing

Make Disciples

"Then Jesus came to them and said, 'All authority in heaven and on earth has been given to me. Therefore go and make disciples of all nations, baptizing them in the name of the Father and of the Son and of the Holy Spirit, and teaching them to obey everything I have commanded you. And surely I am with you always, to the very end of the age.'"

Jesus, Matthew 28:18-20

Would You be Guilty?

If you were arrested and charged with being a Christian, would there be enough evidence to convict you?

Do Not Disparage

Instead of speaking bad about a person or gossiping about their weaknesses, declare this:

"They are doing the best they can with what they know and they'll get better."

Don G. Castleberry, *Founder of Freedom in Jesus Prison Ministries*

Faith acronym:

Forsaking All in Trusting Him.

Faith versus Fear

Faith is developed by meditating on God's Word.

Fear is developed by meditating on Satan's lies.

Such fearful meditation is called "worrying".

Don't do it!

Kindness

You cannot do a kindness too soon, for you never know how soon it will be before it's too late.

Fear God

The person who fears God need not fear anything else; but the person who does not fear God is vulnerable to fearing everything else!

Caring

It's none of my business what someone thinks about me.

It's not even my business if someone cares about me or not.

My business is caring about them.

Witnessing

Are we as Christians willing to do for the truth what some religious cults are willing to do for a lie?

More Grace

While God opposes the proud, He increases grace to the humble (James 4:6-8).

Five steps to obtaining more grace:

1. "Submit yourselves to God."
2. "Resist the devil" in whatever form he appears.
3. "Draw nigh to God" in worship, praise and thanksgiving, prayer and fasting, and in fellowship with the Holy Spirit and the Word.
4. "Cleanse your hands" by confessing sin and getting your outward life right before God; and,
5. "Purify your hearts" by letting God cleanse your inner life and thoughts.

Courage

You weren't ashamed of being a sinner, so don't be ashamed of being a Christian.

Rest

"If you look at the world you'll be distressed;

If you look within you'll be depressed;

But if you look at Christ, you'll be at rest."

Corrie Ten Boom

Be with Jesus

"When they saw the courage of Peter and John and realized that they were unschooled, ordinary men, they were astonished and they took note that these men had been with Jesus."

Luke the Physician, Acts 4:13

Your Gift

What you are is God's gift to you; what you do with who you are is your gift to God.

Great Commitment

A great commitment to the Greatest Commandment and the Great Commission will make you a great Christian.

Make Love Allowances

"Live with patience, bearing with one another, making love allowances for each other's mistakes."

Don G. Castleberry, *Founder of Freedom in Jesus Prison Ministries*

The Fear of the Lord (Reverence)

True reverence and the fear of the Lord are closely related. There are three aspects of the fear of the Lord:

1. Fear of punishment – Both believers and non-believers should experience this type of fear. Hebrews 10:31: "For it is a fearful thing to fall into the hands of the living God."

2. Fear of damaging God's reputation – If people consider us to be believers in the Lord and they see, or hear about, us acting in a non-Christian way, it would damage God's reputation in their eyes.

3. Fear of breaking an intimate relationship with the Lord – We should avoid doing anything that would negatively impact our close and intimate relationship with the Lord. This is the beginning of wisdom and brings riches, honor and life (Proverbs 9:10; 22:14).

Determining Right from Wrong

If something is not expressly stated in God's Word, how do I determine right and wrong?

"In everything we say, do, think or enjoy, we must ask the following:

1. Can it be done to God's Glory?
2. Can it be done in the Name of the Lord Jesus, asking His blessing on it?
3. Can it be done while sincerely giving thanks to God?
4. Is it a Christ-like action?
5. Will it weaken the sincere conviction of other Christians?
6. Will it weaken my desire for intimate fellowship with Christ, God's Word, or prayer?
7. Will it weaken or hinder my witness for Christ?"

Life in the Spirit Study Bible, by Zondervan

The Way

We don't need to see the way if we are following the One Who is the Way.

Trusting God

If you know that God's hand is in everything, you can leave everything in God's hands.

Tragedies

"Just because God works incredible good out of unspeakable tragedies doesn't mean He orchestrates the tragedies. Don't ever assume that His using something means He caused it; or, that He needs it to accomplish His purposes."

William P. Young, *The Shack*

Forgiveness and Kindness

"Every time we forgive, the universe changes; every time you reach out and touch a heart or life, the world changes; with every kindness and service, seen or unseen, God's purposes are accomplished and nothing will ever be the same again."

William P. Young, *The Shack*

Who You Are

"You will never understand who you are until you understand who God is. Why? Because God made us; and, He made us in His own image."

Billy Graham, *The Journey*

God is a Spirit

"God is a Spirit, infinite, eternal, and unchangeable in His Being, wisdom, power, holiness, justice, goodness, and truth. He is the Great Designer."

Billy Graham, *The Journey*

God's Friend

"The greatest discovery you will ever make is: You were created to know God and to be His friend forever."

Billy Graham, *The Journey*

Walking with Christ

"'Becoming' a Christian takes only a single step; 'Being' a Christian means walking with Christ the rest of your life."

Billy Graham, *The Journey*

Internal Life

"I need Jesus Christ for my eternal life, and the Holy Spirit of God for my internal life!"

Billy Graham, *The Journey*

Fully Forgiven

"Sin breaks our fellowship with God, but it does not end our relationship. We are still His children, even when we disobey. We feel guilty and ashamed, and sometimes we simply want to hide, but God still loves us and He wants to forgive us and welcome us back. The only sin God cannot forgive is the sin of refusing His forgiveness. When you sin, don't excuse it or ignore it or blame it on someone else. Admit it... repent of it... and then rejoice that God has fully forgiven you."

Billy Graham, *The Journey*

Spiritual Beings

We are not human beings going through a temporary spiritual experience; rather, we are spiritual beings going through a temporary human experience.

Storms

God does not always calm the storm, sometimes He calms the child and lets the storms rage on.

Trusting God

When it comes to trusting God, there are two kinds of Christians:

1. Some Christians trust God only if He gives them what *they* think is best.
2. Other Christians trust God no matter what happens to them.

What kind of Christian are you?

God's Love

If you are going to be a successful Christian, you must live daily in God's love for you, not in your love for Him. His love is perfect, strong, pure and complete. Yours is none of that when compared to His love.

Direction

Direction, not intention, determines destination.

Your Future

Never be afraid to entrust your unknown future to the all-knowing God.

God Can Do It

When we do what we can, God will do what we cannot.

Forward Looking

Regret is backward looking, depression is inward looking, but hope is forward looking. Everyone needs a measure of hope to survive.

Make it Right

The only way to make things right is to admit you've been wrong.

Depend on God

God does not intend us to become stronger so we can depend on ourselves, He brings us to the end of ourselves so that we will depend solely on Him.

Tell Somebody

Tell somebody about the One Who is Somebody!

God-consciousness

"The best answer to self-consciousness is God-consciousness. When I concern myself, not with the perceived inequities and injustices I face but rather with ministering the things that matter to God, I feel myself feeling abundantly privileged and blessed. What changed? It was my vision. The surest way to lift a person's spirit is to lift his focus.

"When I look not only to the things of God, but to God Himself, I find that I have more reasons to rejoice than I have to mourn. I possess more than I've lost. I have more in my hand than has slipped through my fingers. I have more to thank God for than to petition Him for."

F.B. Meyer, *London Pastor*

The Holy Spirit

Romans 8 clearly defines the work of the Holy Spirit:

- There is power over sin (verses 1-2).
- He will fulfill the law (verses 3-4).
- He will give you the mind of God (verses 5-8).
- He will give you righteousness (verses 9-10).
- He will give life and health to your body (verse 11).
- He will bring death to self (verses 12-14).
- He will testify of your salvation (verses 15-16).

Without a fresh, daily anointing of the Holy Spirit, it is impossible to:

- Know God (Eph. 5:18; Rom. 8:16).
- Understand the Kingdom of God (Luke 17:21; Rom. 14:17).
- Know the Truth (John 14:26; 1 John 5:6; John 16:13).
- Stay free from sin (Rom. 8:2).

- Pray with power (Rom. 8:26).
- Have a faith-filled life (2 Cor. 5:7).
- Live an unshakeable, established Christian life (Eph. 3:16-17; Lam. 3:22-25)

Be Witnesses

"On one occasion, while he was eating with them, he gave them this command: 'Do not leave Jerusalem, but wait for the gift my Father promised, which you have heard me speak about. For John baptized with water, but in a few days you will be baptized with the Holy Spirit… you will receive power when the Holy Spirit comes on you; and you will be my witnesses in Jerusalem, and in all Judea and Samaria, and to the ends of the earth.'"

Jesus, *Acts 1:4-5, 8*

Ministry

"Take care of the depth of your ministry, and God will take care of the breadth of it."

Dr. John MacArthur

Take God as He Is

"Much of our difficulty as seeking Christians stems from our unwillingness to take God as He is and adjust our lives accordingly. We insist upon trying to modify Him to bring Him nearer to our own image of Him."

A.W. Tozer

Forget Your Troubles

What a wonderful world this would be if we could forget our troubles as easily as we forget our blessings.

Excellence

Excellence is the result of:

- Caring more than others think is wise;

- Risking more than others think is safe;

- Dreaming more than others think is practical; and,

- Expecting more than others think is possible.

Love

To know love, open your heart to Jesus.

To show love, open your heart to others.

God wants to love others through you.

Going through Hell

When you are "catching hell", don't hold it.

When you are "going through hell", don't stop!

Repentance

True repentance is a change in your thinking about God that leads to a change in the way you live.

Working in You

Christianity is not you working for or in God, it is God working in you. It is not a religion, it is the person of Jesus Christ!

If Nothing Changes

We need to quit asking God to change our circumstances and start asking Him to change us! Our circumstances are often brought on by our actions. Our actions change when our thinking changes. Our thinking changes as the Word and prayer transform us. But, if nothing changes, nothing changes! It isn't what happens to you, it's what happens in you.

Forgetting the Past

"Line yourself up with the Word of God. Stop believing how you feel. Stop believing what you've done before. Don't believe more in your mistakes than you do in the Word of God. He says you're led by the Spirit. He says you hear His voice and follow."

Karen Jensen

Faith and Obedience

"Faith and obedience are inescapably related. There is no saving faith in God apart from obedience to God, and there can be no Godly obedience without Godly faith."

Dr. John MacArthur

Glorify and Display

We as believers are here to glorify God. We are here for God to display the superiority of a life lived in God.

Nearness to God

"Nearness to God brings likeness to God. The more you see God, the more of God will be seen in you."

Charles Spurgeon

We Need the Spirit

"Sometimes we don't realize how much we need the Holy Spirit. Though we acknowledge that salvation is accomplished by Christ alone, how many of us feel as if living the Christian life is now up to us? But self-reliance is a recipe for failure. Only when you know you can't, will you find out He can!"

Dr. Charles Stanley

The Root

"Faith is the root of all good works. A root that produces nothing is dead."

Thomas Wilson

What is God Up To Now?

Sometimes we ask, "What is God up to now?"
God does not reject our honest questions. It's our
arrogant demands that He refuses.

Love in Deed

Love in deed is love indeed.

Don't Keep It

The good news of Christ is too good to keep it to yourself!

Truth

The truth of the Father is revealed by the Son,
and received by the Spirit.

Glorify and Enjoy

"The chief end of man is to glorify God by enjoying Him forever."

John Piper

Care for Others

People don't care what you know until they know that you care.

Jesus Loves Me

"The greatest truth of all eternity is this: Jesus loves me this I know, for the Bible tells me so!' You will never outgrow your need to receive and release the love of God. Everyone everywhere has a love deficit-so watch the love of Christ change the world, starting with me and with you!"

Charles Finney

Plant Seeds

Don't judge each day by the harvest you reap, but by the seeds you plant.

Your Efforts

"When you commit to sharing eternal hope your efforts will bear fruit (Colossians 1:5-6). When you serve God, you are never at risk of wasting your life. Your efforts will produce hope that lasts for eternity, and sharing the love of Christ fills your life with meaning."

Dr. Morris Sheets

Identity Crisis

You are not what you do (your "role"). God gives you your true "identity" in Christ which you obtained through God's grace. Once accepted by you it cannot be taken away, cannot be stolen (identity theft).

However, in error, we sometimes give it away. God will not take it away (Ephesians 3:14-21).

Don't let Satan or anyone else lie to you about your true identity. It is "in Christ" where our true identity lies forever. A man is lost when he does not know where he is, but he is truly lost when he doesn't know who he is. Thank God, He allows us to re-claim our identity when we finally "come to ourselves" like the Prodigal Son and return in true repentance to Him! God is the answer to any identity crisis.

God was with Him

"You know the message God sent to the people of Israel, announcing the good news of peace through Jesus Christ, who is Lord of all. You know what has happened throughout the province of Judea, beginning in Galilee after the baptism that John preached— how God anointed Jesus of Nazareth with the Holy Spirit and power, and how he went around doing good and healing all who were under the power of the devil, because God was with him."

Peter the Apostle, *Acts 10:36-38*

Nothing to Worry About

There are only two things to worry about: either you are sick or you are well. If you're well, then there's nothing to worry about. If you're sick, you have two things to worry about... either you live or you die. If you live, you have nothing to worry about. If you die, you only have two things to worry about. Either you go to Heaven or you go to Hell. If you go to Heaven, you have nothing to worry about. But if you go to Hell, you'll be so busy shaking hands with old friends, you won't have time to worry. Therefore, witness to your friends and accept Christ, then when you die there is nothing to worry about.

The Gospel According to You

You are writing a Gospel, a chapter each day,

By the deeds that you do and the words that you say.

Men read what you write, whether faithless or true,

So what is the Gospel, according to you?

You are writing each day a gospel for men.

Make sure that the writing is true.

For the only Gospel that many men heed,

Is the Gospel according to you.

Obedience

Obedience is doing it quickly and quietly.

Delayed obedience is disobedience.

Partial obedience is disobedience.

In your journey of faith, God will not progress you past your last act of disobedience.

Obey and continue your journey.

Changed?

If your faith hasn't changed you, it hasn't saved you!

Endurance

The ultimate test of true Christianity is endurance empowered by the Holy Spirit's indwelling.

Make-believers

"I believe in the security of believers, but I also believe in the insecurity of make-believers!"

J. Vernon McGee

The Tree of Love

"Love for God is the root, and love for neighbors is the fruit of the tree of love. The one cannot exist without the other, but the former is the cause and the latter is the effect."

William Temple

Invest

"You will invest your life in something, or you will throw it away on nothing."

Haddon Robinson

Giant Problems

Don't compare yourself with your giants, compare your giants with God!

Three Things God Doesn't Know

1. He does not know a sin he doesn't hate.
2. He does not know a sinner he doesn't love.
3. He does not know a better day than today to be saved!

Evangelist John Bayer

Obedience

"In many ways, the attitude of obedience is much more vital than the act, because if the attitude is right, the act will naturally follow. But the right action with the wrong attitude is nothing but hypocrisy."

Dr. John MacArthur

A Process

"Ask the God who made you to keep re-making you!"

Norman Vincent Peale

Becoming

"A Christian is never in a state of completion but always in the process of becoming."

Martin Luther

Faith Receives the Impossible

"Faith sees the invisible, believes the incredible, knows the unknowable, and receives the impossible."

Dr. Adrian Rogers, *Adrianisms, Volume 2*

The Love of God

"It has been my one and only business to set forth the love of God to men in Jesus Christ."

Charles Spurgeon

Association

You take on the identity of those you choose to associate with-birds of a feather flock together.

Surrender

We must stop "trying to live for God". Instead, we must let God live through us! The key to all victory in the Christian life is learning how to depend on the Holy Spirit for our strength.

Forgiveness

To enjoy your future, accept God's forgiveness of your past.

The Last Word

The best way to get the last word is to apologize and ask for forgiveness.

Witnessing

"The future is glorious. The best is yet to be, and you and I have the privilege to help hasten the coming of Jesus."

Corrie Ten Boom

Fear of the Lord

The fear of the Lord is a reverent awe of God's power, majesty and holiness. It produces in us a holy fear of transgressing His revealed will; which is essential to gaining a heart of wisdom.

See *Proverbs 1:7*

Humility

Humility is not thinking less of yourself; it is thinking of yourself less. Humility is thinking more of others. Humble people are so focused on serving others, they don't think of themselves. It is the opposite of pride. It is the displacement of self by the enthronement of God. Where God is all, self is nothing.

Pride

Pride involves making the final decision for myself in life, no matter what God says. Also, it is taking credit for something that was really done by God or others.

A Desire to Help

Compassion is an emotion that moves people to the very depth of their being. It involves sorrow felt for another's suffering and misfortune, accompanied by an intense desire to help.

Eternal Hope

The world can neither give nor take away the hope of a Christian. Such hope comes from God, and He will never withdraw it.

A Hardened Heart

A hardened heart is indicated by the failure to respond to a person or a message. It is also to be strong, hard, harsh and severe. It is to deaden or make dull. It includes being obstinate and unresponsive, rebellious, and spiritually insensitive. A hardened heart is unable to understand spiritual truth.

A Message to Share

God gave you a message to share; don't keep it to yourself! The abundant grace and mercy towards

Paul (and us) should encourage us to present the Gospel even to the worst of sinners, confident that God's grace and power can redeem and change their lives also!

See Paul's testimony in *1 Timothy 1:12-17*.

A Glowing Witness

"A Christian with a glowing witness is worth a library full of arguments."

Dr. Adrian Rogers, *Adrianisms, Volume 2*

The Shofar

"In the Old Testament, the ram's horn, or shofar, was blown to:

- Call an assembly to war.
- Call an assembly to worship.
- Stir panic in the camp of the enemy.
- Announce a victory."

Glenn Arekion

All In

"Go all in and all out for the All in All!"

Pastor Mark Batterson, *Going All In*

Our All

"Having made Jesus our all, we will find all in Jesus."

Charles Spurgeon

Step Out

God can correct a mistake, but not inactivity—

step out in faith!

Our Weakness

"Our weakness is not the trouble; the trouble is our unwillingness to acknowledge our weakness."

Chip Brogden

Jesus in You

"All of Heaven is attracted to Jesus in you!"

Graham Cooke

Passions

"God's man is called to invest his passions in the service of life, not invest his life in the service of his passions. God knows we have energy to devote to something, and He designed that energy to put toward knowing and loving Him and His love for us. The objects we worship hijack our souls, morph our characters and transform our conduct."

Every Man Ministries

Forgive

"A Christian who cannot forgive is one who has forgotten how much he has been forgiven."

John Bevere

Judgment

"With hearing comes knowledge. With knowledge comes responsibility. With responsibility comes accountability. With accountability comes overseer judgment. You have heard the Word. What are you doing with it?"

Stephen E. Canup

Stop Using God

We need to stop using God and let Him start using us!

Seven Steps in Counseling Others

Consider these seven steps in mentoring and/or counseling others:

1. Show by your own life.
2. Tell them about Jesus.

3. Pray for them.
4. Encourage and edify them.
5. Love them unconditionally, but speak the truth in love.
6. Point them to the Counselor, the Holy Spirit
7. Let go, and let God be God.

You cannot live their lives for them. Turn them over to God. Trust Him to bring them along. Keep loving them where they're at.

How to Treat Others

"Treat people as if they were what they ought to be, and you help them become what they are capable of being!"

Johann Wolfgang Van Goethe

God Doesn't Cover Up

"The Father doesn't waste His time trying to cover up who we were. Rather, He devotes Himself to uncovering who we truly are, who He made us to be!"

Craig Denison, *First15.org*

Tell Others

"Then, leaving her water jar, the woman went back to the town and said to the people, 'Come, see a man who told me everything I ever did. Could this be the Messiah?'"

The Samaritan Woman, *John 4:28-29*

A Disciple's Prayer of Submission

Father God, I humbly submit myself fully to You and your leadership by Your Holy Spirit.

"Holy, Holy, Holy is the Lord God Almighty, who was, and is, and is to come...You are worthy, O Lord, to receive all glory, honor and praise."

Lord, please forgive me for both my willful and my unintentional sins. Help me to freely and fully forgive others as You forgive me.

Father, I submit willingly and completely to your Hand as The Potter. Re-make me into the person You want me to be for the plan You have for me in Your perfect will. As You do, conform me to the image of Jesus by the sanctifying work of Your Holy Spirit.

Father, by Your grace help me to always be a grateful, humble heir of all Your promises; an obedient, faithful servant of all Your commands; a persistent, bold witness of Your salvation through Jesus; and, a loving, trusting child full of Your love. I surrender to Your Holy Spirit's leadership.

Let me be patient and persevering in prayer, ever watchful and responsive for opportunities to bless others as You have blessed me. Empower me Father with Your grace, through the Spirit of Jesus in me, to diligently seek You and Your eternal Kingdom, so that I will not be distracted and overcome with the temptations and temporary pleasures of this alien world. In everything I think, say and do today, Father, let me continually glorify and honor You.

I love You, Jesus. I praise You and adore You for first loving me. Thank You for being made sin for me so that I am made righteous in You. Please love and bless others through me today as I seek to know and do Your perfect will for my life. I want to be led today by Your Holy Spirit in me.

In the power of the blood of Jesus, and the authority of His Name I pray. Amen.

Prayer and Devotion

Abide in Jesus

"If you remain in me and my words remain in you, ask whatever you wish, and it will be done for you. This is to my Father's glory, that you bear much fruit, showing yourselves to be my disciples."

Jesus, *John 15:7-8*

A Prayer

Father God, please give me a passion for your Word, and help me be obedient to your Will. I want others to see your work in me. Having been created for good works, I pray these works will pass the test of fire in your Kingdom. Examine my motives and make my life a magnet to draw many to you. I desire You to receive all the Glory. In the Name of Jesus, Amen.

Ephesians 2:10; Proverbs 16:2; 1 Corinthians 3:11-13; Revelation 19:1, 5-7

Satan Trembles

Satan trembles when he sees the weakest Christian on his knees.

Trust in God

Oh Lord, I choose to trust in Who You are rather than in who I am. In Jesus' Name, Amen

Fully Devoted

God takes full responsibility for the life that is fully devoted to Him.

On Your Knees

You cannot stumble if you are on your knees; you cannot cry if you are looking up!

Two or More Agree

"Again, truly I tell you that if two of you on earth agree about anything they ask for, it will be done for them by my Father in heaven. For where two or three gather in my name, there am I with them."

Jesus, *Matthew 18:19-20*

In God's Hands

What we have in our hand we will lose, but what we put in God's hand is never lost!

Alone with God

"No person can expect to make progress in holiness who is not often and long alone with God."

Andrew Murray

God's Presence

God's presence is a life preserver that keeps the soul from sinking in a sea of trouble.

Devotion

"The dictionary defines 'devotion' as religious fervor; an act of prayer or private worship; a religious exercise separate from corporate worship. Devotion is prayer, reverence, constancy and passion.

"My definition of 'devotion' is taking time to sit at the feet of Jesus and to listen to his Word because I love Him. Living with a heart of devotion is about giving Him the best of my time and thoughts so that as I go about my day, my heart is centered on and devoted to Christ."

Cynthia Heald, *Decision Magazine, April, 2010*

A.S.A.P.

Always say a prayer!

Prayer should be our first response rather than our last resort. So before you do anything else, remember to A.S.A.P. – always say a prayer... as soon as possible!

The Blue-print

"Prayer is the blue-print for a successful life."

Joyce Meyer

The ACTS of Prayer

Four important areas of prayer:

- Adoration – Reflect on God Himself. Praise Him for His attributes, His majesty, His gift of Christ.

- Confession – admit to God you have sinned. Be honest and humble. Remember, He knows you and loves you.

- Thanksgiving – Tell God how grateful you are for everything He has given you, even the unpleasant things. Your thankfulness will help you see His purposes.

- Supplication – Make specific requests. Pray for others first, then for yourself.

From a teaching on prayer from the Rock of Ages Prison Ministry

Thanksgiving and Praise

"Thanksgiving enjoys the gift.

Praise enjoys the Giver."

Dr. Adrian Rogers, *Adrianisms,* **Volume 2**

Reach Up

"Oh Lord Jesus, help us to know that when we reach up to thee, thou art reaching down to us."

Peter Marshall

Worship

If God was small enough for us to understand,

He wouldn't be big enough for us to worship.

Don't Worry

Let your faith overcome your fear, and God will turn your worry into worship!

Our First Resource

God and prayer should be our first resource, not our last resort!

Be Sure to Ask

"Satan can't keep God from answering our prayers, but he will keep us from asking."

Dr. Adrian Rogers, *Adrianisms, Volume 2*

Move God

"Only God can move mountains, but faith and prayer can move God."

E.M. Bounds

Why?

"I am truly grateful that faith enables me to move past the question of 'Why'."

Zig Ziglar

Abomination

An abomination to God is that which defames or pollutes what is Holy.

Prayerlessness

"Prayerlessness is a spirit of independence from God."

Dr. Adrian Rogers, *Adrianisms, Volume 2*

Pray Not to Be

"Pray to desire not to be esteemed, not to be secure and not to be in control."

A Trappist Monk, *per Derek Prince*

A Prayer for Forgiving Myself and the Healing of My Past

Heavenly Father, I come to you in the mighty Name of Jesus, and I give You my past. I repent of my un-forgiveness towards myself, and I confess it as a sin. I ask You, Father, to heal my memories; to remedy the wrongs of my past; and, to turn my past into something that can be used for good in my future and in the future of others. I choose to give up my claim to my past and turn it completely over to Jesus Christ. Through Your Holy Spirit help me forgive myself and others, and put the past behind me forever. Thank you that I am a new creation walking forward into my future in Christ. I believe I have received what I've asked you for Father, and I thank you for it in Jesus' name. Amen.

Seek God Early

"The men who have done the most for God
in this world have been early on their knees.
He who fritters away the early morning, its
opportunity and freshness, in other pursuits than
seeking God will make poor headway seeking
Him the rest of the day. If God is not first in our
thoughts and efforts in the morning, He will be
in last place the remainder of the day."

E.M. Bounds, *Power through Prayer*

Meet with God

"As the deer pants for streams of water,
so my soul pants for you, my God.
My soul thirsts for God, for the living God.
When can I go and meet with God?"

Psalm 42:1-2

I Praise You Lord

I praise you Lord from my soul. From my inmost being I praise your Holy name. I praise you Lord from my soul. I will not forget all your benefits – you forgive all my sins and heal all my diseases. You redeemed my life from the pit and crowned me with your love and compassion. You satisfy my desires with good things so that my youth is renewed like an eagle's. In Jesus' Name, amen.

Personalized from Psalm 103:1-5

In the Shelter of the Most High

As I dwell in the shelter of the Most High I will rest in the shadow of the Almighty. I will say of you Lord, "You are my refuge and my fortress. You are my God and I will trust in you." Surely you will save me from the fowler's snare and from the deadly pestilence. You will cover me with your feathers, and under your wings I will find refuge; your faithfulness will be my shield and rampart.

I will not fear the terror of night nor the arrow that flies by day, nor the pestilence that stalks in the darkness, nor the plague that destroys at midday. A thousand may fall at my side, ten thousand by my right hand, but it will not come near me.

I will observe with my eyes and see the punishment of the wicked. I will make the Most High my dwelling – the Lord is my refuge – so that no harm will befall me, no disaster will come near my tent. God, you will command your angels concerning me to guard me in all my ways; they will lift me up in their hands, so that I will not strike my foot against a stone. I will tread upon the lion and the cobra; I will trample the great lion and the serpent.

Lord, you said because I love you, you will rescue me. You will protect me, for I acknowledge your name. I will call upon you and you will answer me; you will be with me in trouble, you will deliver me and honor me. With long life will you satisfy me and show me your salvation. In Jesus' Name, amen.

Personalized from Psalm 91

No Weapon will Prevail Against Me

No weapon forged against me will prevail and I will refute every tongue that accuses me. This is my heritage as a servant of the Lord, and this is my vindication from you. In Jesus' Name, amen.

Personalized from Isaiah 54:17

A Spirit of Wisdom and Revelation

I keep asking that you, God of my Lord Jesus Christ, my glorious Father, may give me the Spirit of wisdom and revelation that I may know you better. I pray also that the eyes of my heart may be enlightened in order that I may know the hope to which you have called me, the riches of your glorious inheritance in the saints, and your incomparably great power for us who believe. That power is like the working of your mighty strength, which you exerted in Christ when you raised Him from the dead and seated Him at your right hand in heavenly realms, far above all rule and authority, power and dominion, and every title that can be given, not only in the present age but also in the one to come. And you, God, placed all things under His feet and appointed Him to be over everything for the church, which is His body, the fullness of Him who fills everything in every way. In Jesus' Name, amen.

Personalized from Ephesians 1:17-23

Rooted and Established in Love

I pray that out of your glorious riches you may strengthen me with power through your Spirit in my inner being, so that Christ may dwell in my heart through faith. And I pray that as I am rooted and established in love, I may have power, together with all the saints, to grasp how wide and long and high and deep is the love of Christ, and that I may know this love that surpasses knowledge – that I may be filled to the measure of all your fullness.

Now to you, God, who is able to do immeasurably more than all I ask or imagine, according to your power that is at work within me, to you be glory in the church and in Christ Jesus throughout all generations, forever and ever! In Jesus' Name, amen.

Personalized from Ephesians 3:16-21

That My Love May Abound

This also is my prayer: that my love may abound more and more in knowledge and depth of insight, so that I may be able to discern what is best and may be pure and blameless until the day of Christ, filled with the fruit of righteousness that comes through Jesus Christ – to the glory and praise of you, God. In Jesus' Name, amen.

Personalized from Philippians 1:9-11

A Life Worthy of the Lord Jesus

I pray that you fill me with the knowledge of your will through all spiritual wisdom and understanding. I pray this in order that I may live a life worthy of the Lord Jesus and please Him in every way: bearing fruit in every good work, growing in the knowledge of you, God, so that I may be strengthened with all power according to your glorious might so that I may have great endurance and patience and joyfully give you thanks. In Jesus' Name, amen.

Personalized from Colossians 1:9b-11

Salvation

God Loved and Gave

"For God so loved the world that he gave his one and only Son, that whoever believes in him shall not perish but have eternal life. For God did not send his Son into the world to condemn the world, but to save the world through him."

Jesus, *John 3:16-17*

Salvation

The Greek word most often translated into English in our Bible as "salvation" is "sozo". This Greek word means to be saved, healed, delivered, preserved, made whole, and be put into right relationship with God, with the implication that the condition before was one of grave danger. That's good news!

The "Roman Road to Salvation"

Explaining these scriptures can lead someone to make a salvation decision:

- Romans 3:10 "As it is written, 'There is no one righteous, not even one...'"

- Romans 3:23 "for all have sinned and fall short of the glory of God."

- Romans 5:12 "Therefore, just as sin entered the world through one man, and death through sin, and in this way death came to all people, because all sinned—"

- Romans 6:23 "For the wages of sin is death, but the gift of God is eternal life in Christ Jesus our Lord."

- Romans 5:8 "But God demonstrates his own love for us in this: While we were still sinners, Christ died for us."

- Romans 10:9-10 "If you declare with your mouth, 'Jesus is Lord,' and believe in your heart that God raised him from the dead, you will be saved. For it is with your heart that you believe and are justified, and it is with your mouth that you profess your faith and are saved."

- Romans 10:13 "...for, 'Everyone who calls on the name of the Lord will be saved.'"

- Romans 6:23 "For the wages of sin is death, but the gift of God is eternal life in Christ Jesus our Lord."

Calvary

"Calvary: Earth's greatest tragedy, Heaven's greatest triumph."

Dr. Adrian Rogers, *Adrianisms, Volume 2*

Jesus offers me:

- Forgiveness for my past.

- Peace for my present.

- Hope for my future.

Find the Lost

"For the lost to be found, the found must go find the lost."

Don G. Castleberry, *Founder of Freedom in Jesus Prison Ministries*

The Gospel

The history of the Gospel is His-Story for His Glory.

- Christ died for our sins according to the Scriptures.

- He was buried, and rose again on the 3rd day, according to the Scriptures.

- Men and women are saved by faith and not by works of the law.

- To as many as would receive Him, He gave the right to become the sons of God, even to those who do nothing more nor less than believe on Him.

- Be it known unto you that through this man is preached the remission of sin.

- Believe on the Lord Jesus Christ and you shall be saved.

- There is no other Name under Heaven given among men whereby we must be saved.

- See John 3:16; 1 Corinthians 15:1-11; Colossians 1:15-23; Isaiah 53; Romans 10:15; Acts 8:30-35; Psalm 22; Philippians 2:5-11; Acts 10:38-43; Acts 5:30-32; Acts 2:22-24, 32-33; Hebrews 1:1-3; 1 Timothy 3:16; John 1:1-5, 10-14.

Security

Through salvation:

Our past has been forgiven;

Our present is given meaning; and,

Our future is secured.

Key Definitions

Justice is getting what we deserve.

Mercy is being spared what we deserve.

Grace is being given what we do not deserve.

Our Shepherd

The Lamb who died to save us is the Shepherd who lives to lead us.

Rescued

Those rescued from sin are best able to rescue those in sin.

The Church

The Church is not a collection of perfect saints,

but a gathering of forgiven sinners.

Sinless

A Christian is not sinless, but he does sin less.

Baptism

"Baptism, whether a spoonful or a tankful, can never

save anybody. You are saved by trusting Jesus."

Dr. Adrian Rogers, *Adrianisms,* **Volume 2**

God's Love

God loves each one of us as if there were only one of us to love.

Deliverance

The Cross delivers us from the penalty of sin.

The Resurrection delivers us from the power of sin.

Someday we will be delivered from the presence of sin.

J. Vernon Mcgee

Criticism

People often criticize "the Church" and Christian people. We must realize that all Christians are far from being perfect. They all make mistakes. But one thing is certain: you will never be able to find anything wrong with Jesus Christ. He is the perfect Son of God. He is the one Who wants to change your life and give you everlasting life.

Worthy of Love

"Jesus has judged us worthy of love, even though it cost Him everything. He chose the way of the Cross where mercy triumphs over justice because of love."

William P. Young, *The Shack*

Eternal Transformation

"Jesus didn't come to make you a nicer person. He came to radically, dramatically, and eternally transform you."

Dr. Adrian Rogers, *Adrianisms, Volume 2*

God's Love is Bigger

"God's love is a lot bigger than our own stupidity. He uses our choices (even when we're wrong) to work perfectly into His purposes. Many of us end up locking ourselves into a very small place with a monster that will ultimately betray us; and, that will not fill or deliver what we thought it would. Imprisoned with such a terror, we once again have the opportunity to return to God. The very treasure we trusted in becomes our undoing. The consequences of our selfishness are part of the process that brings us to the end of our delusions, and helps us find our way back to God."

William P. Young, *The Shack*

No Other Name

"Jesus is 'the stone you builders rejected, which has become the cornerstone.' Salvation is found in no one else, for there is no other name under heaven given to mankind by which we must be saved."

Peter the Apostle, Acts 4:11-12

He is No Fool

"He is no fool who gives up what he cannot keep (this temporary life) to gain what he cannot lose (eternal life with Christ)."

Jim Elliot, 20th century martyr

"Religion"

The difference between "Religion" and Christianity?

"Religion" is man's attempt to reach God, while Jesus is God's attempt to reach man.

A Futile Search

"Without God, we are empty and restless. We are incomplete without God. If we leave Him out of our lives, we have an empty place in our souls, a yearning deep inside us that only God can satisfy. No matter how hard we try, if we ignore God that hollow place stays with us, and our search for lasting peace and happiness will be futile."

Billy Graham, *The Journey*

Jesus is the Way

"Jesus doesn't show us the way to Heaven. He is the way to Heaven."

Dr. Adrian Rogers, *Adrianisms, Volume 2*

Lord of Hope

We hold onto our hope in the Lord, because we belong to the Lord of our Hope.

Know

No God, no hope. Know God, know hope.

No Jesus, no peace. Know Jesus, know peace.

Hope for the World

"Outside the resurrection of Jesus Christ, I know of no other hope for mankind."

Konrad Adenauer, *U.S. Ambassador to Germany, in a discussion with Billy Graham*

No Sacrifice Too Great

If Jesus Christ is God and He died for me, then no sacrifice can be too great for me to make for Him!

Prepared Place

God has a place prepared for prepared children!

Find Jesus First

Many people try to find themselves before they find Jesus, but they need to know that when they find Jesus, they will find themselves.

Salvation

"Salvation doesn't come from following the life of Christ but receiving the death of Christ."

Dr. Adrian Rogers, *Adrianisms,* **Volume 2**

Baptism

Baptism should be seen as an outward act by which we publicly identify with Christ and His Church. The Bible makes it clear that baptism is an evidence of salvation and forgiveness, not a requirement for it. It is an evidence of repentance and forgiveness, not a condition for it.

These factors show that water baptism is not essential to salvation:

- Abraham was forgiven before he was circumcised, apart from any rite or ceremony (Romans 4:9-10).

- Jesus declared people forgiven before they were baptized (Matt. 9:1-7; Luke 7:36-50; Luke 18:9-14; Luke 19:1-9; John 8:1-12).

- Cornelius and his family received the Holy Spirit before baptism (Acts 10:44-48).

- The Bible shows that forgiveness and salvation are received by faith (John 3:16; Rom. 5:1; Rom. 10:1-13; Eph. 2:10).

Proof of the Resurrection

"People will die for their religious beliefs if they sincerely believe they are true (e.g. Muslims, Jim Jones, David Koresh followers), but people won't die for their religious beliefs if they know their beliefs are false. All the Apostles except John died horrible martyrs' deaths rather than abandon their belief and faith in Jesus."

Martyrdom of Apostles

A Great Need

"I have a great need for Christ; I have a great Christ for my need."

Charles Spurgeon

Give Yourself

Ask God, Who gave Himself completely for you, to help you give yourself completely to Him.

Saved By Grace

"Not only is a sinner saved by grace through faith, but the saved sinner lives by grace. Grace is a way to life and a way of life!"

J. Vernon McGee

Horrors of Hell

The same Christ who talks about the glories of Heaven also describes the horrors of Hell.

By Grace

Because of God's mercy, He overlooks sin for a time.

Because of God's justice, He demands a price be paid for your sin.

Because of God's grace, He paid the price Himself with His Son.

But you must receive Christ into your life as your savior through faith.

So, by grace you are saved!

The Way

"Jesus answered, 'I am the way and the truth and the life. No one comes to the Father except through me.'"

Jesus, John 14:6

Love Born at Calvary

Love that is born at Calvary bears and forbears, gives and forgives.

Regeneration

Regeneration is a re-creating of spiritual life in the human heart by God the Holy Spirit, imparting eternal life to the believer's heart. It comes to those who repent of sin, turn to God, and put their faith in the Lord Jesus Christ alone for salvation.

Salvation

Salvation has these shades of meaning: deliverance, bringing safely through, and keeping from harm. In the New Testament it is described as "The Way", or road that leads through life to eternal fellowship with God in heaven.

Eternal Hope

"Eternal hope is having assurance that we have already been saved in Christ Jesus, our hope (and confidence) is that we will not see spiritual death but have eternal life. It is a personal hope founded on a personal conviction and is given to, or worked in us, by the Holy Spirit.

"A Christian's hope is made of:

- The Christian believes that Christ came into the world to save sinners,

- He trusts Christ to save him,

- He hopes that when Christ comes he shall reign with Him,

- That when the trumpet blows he shall rise with Christ, and,

- That in Heaven he shall have a secure dwelling place at the right hand of the Father."

Charles Spurgeon

The Battle was Won

The battle was won at the Cross. Jesus laid down His will. He took on the Father's will. He was obedient, even to death on the Cross.

Evidence of Christ's Life in Us

"What is the evidence of Christ's life in us? A love that consumes us; a joy that sustains us; a hope that brightens our outlook; a purity that maintains our holiness; and, a commitment that makes others want to follow our Savior."

Dr. David Jeremiah

God's Symphony of Salvation

"God plays the symphony of our salvation in three movements. Each movement is associated with a different person of the Trinity: the Father, the Son and the Holy Spirit. First, there is the work of God the Father in administering our salvation. The Father is the One Who organizes and oversees the plan of salvation. Second, there is the work of God the Son in accomplishing our salvation. Jesus is the One Who died for our sins and rose again to give us eternal life. Third, there is the work of God the Holy Spirit in applying our salvation. The Spirit is the One Who takes what Jesus Christ has done and makes it ours. This is the Plan, and the Triune God has been working it out since before the beginning of time."

Philip Rykin and Michael Lebvre

Heaven

"Heaven is a place for those who love the Lord; where everything revolves around His majesty, power, glory and presence (Revelation 19:1-7). Every person there will praise and worship Him. If someone refused to honor and serve Him here on Earth, they won't like Heaven at all. In fact, they will be completely out of place there."

Dr. Charles Stanley

The Gospel in a Nutshell

The Christian message can be summarized as follows:

- The greatest ethic is love.

- Where love is a reality, freedom has to be given.
- Where there is freedom, there will always be the possibility of sin.
- Where there is sin, there is need of a savior.
- Where there is a savior, there is the hope of redemption.

Only in the Judeo-Christian worldview does this sequence find its total expression and answer. That in a nutshell is the entire Gospel story, and that is uniquely true of the message of Jesus Christ!

Humble Hearts

"The miracle working power of God the Holy Spirit works in helpless, hungry, hopeless, hurting, homesick, humble hearts!"

Stephen E. Canup

Bankrupt

"The sin of the guilty must be paid by the innocent because the guilty are bankrupt!"

Pastor Jared Baker

F.A.I.T.H.

"Forsaking all I take Him."

Glenda Jackson

F.E.A.R.

False evidence appearing real.

Salvation Directed Questions

- Do you realize you're lost?

- Are you willing to be found?
- Are you ready to turn from your sin?

What Must I Do to be Saved?

"To the question, what must I do to be saved:

- Surrender to Jesus Christ.
- Get to know God personally.
- Grow to become like Him."

A.W. Tozer

The Gospel Message

"The Gospel message is not just a message of pardon; but it is a message of repentance. It is a message of atonement; but it is also a message of temperance and righteousness and godliness in this present world. It tells us that we must accept a savior; but it tells us also we must deny ungodliness and worldly lusts. The Gospel message includes the idea of amendment (change), of separation from the world, of cross-carrying and loyalty to the Kingdom of God even unto death."

A.W. Tozer

See Titus 2:11-12

No Other Savior

"'You are my witnesses,' declares the Lord,
'and my servant whom I have chosen,
so that you may know and believe me
and understand that I am he.
Before me no god was formed,
nor will there be one after me.
I, even I, am the Lord,
and apart from me there is no savior.'"

Jehovah, *Isaiah 43:10-11*

You Can Have "The Real Thing"

"The Real Thing" has nothing to do with "religion." Rather, it is an intimate personal relationship with our Heavenly Father, because of the finished work of Jesus at the Cross. The Holy Spirit comes and seals us as His very own, and begins an ongoing work in us to conform us to the image of Christ Jesus.

You can begin this exciting and abundant life today. It will continue throughout all eternity.

First, acknowledge and confess that you have sinned against God.

Second, renounce your sins – determine that you are not going back to them. Turn away from sin. Turn to God.

Third, by faith receive Christ into your heart. Surrender your life completely to Him. He will come to live in your heart by the Holy Spirit.

You can do this right now.

Start by simply talking to God. You can pray a prayer like this:

"Oh God, I am a sinner. I'm sorry for my sin. I want to turn from my sin. Please forgive me. I believe Jesus Christ is Your Son; I believe He died on the Cross for my sin and You raised Him to life. I want to trust Him as my Savior and follow Him

as my Lord from this day forward, forevermore. Lord Jesus, I put my trust in You and surrender my life to You. Please come into my life and fill me with your Holy Spirit. In Jesus' Name. Amen."

If you just said this prayer, and you meant it with all your heart, we believe you just got Saved and are now Born Again in Christ Jesus as a totally new person.

"Therefore, if anyone is in Christ, he is a new creation; the old has gone, the new has come!" (II Corinthians 5:17)

We urge you to go "all in and all out for the All in All"! (Pastor Mark Batterson, *All In*)

We suggest you follow the Lord in water baptism at your earliest opportunity. Water baptism is an outward symbol of the inward change that follows your salvation and re-birth.

The grace of God Himself gives you the desire and ability to surrender completely to the Holy Spirit's work in and through you (Philippians 2:13).

The Baptism in the Holy Spirit is His empowerment for you.

You Can Receive the Baptism in the Holy Spirit

The Baptism in the Holy Spirit is a separate experience and a Holy privilege granted to those who ask. This is God's own power to enable you to live an abundant, overcoming life. The Bible says it is the same power that raised Jesus from the dead (Romans 1:4; 8:11; II Cor. 4:13-14; 1 Peter 3:18).

Have you asked the Father for Jesus to baptize you (immerse you) in the Holy Spirit (Luke 3:16)? If you ask the Father, He will give Him to you (Luke 11:13). Have you allowed the "rivers of living water" to flow from within you (John 7:38-39)? Our Father desires for us to walk in all His fullness by His Holy Spirit.

The power to witness, and live your life the way Jesus did in intimate relationship with the Father, comes from asking Jesus to baptize you in the Holy Spirit. To receive this baptism, pray along these lines:

Abba Father and my Lord Jesus,

Thank you for giving me your Spirit to live inside me. I am saved by grace through faith in Jesus. I ask you now to baptize me in the Holy Ghost with Your fire and power. I fully receive it through faith just like I did my salvation. Now, Holy Spirit, come and rise up within me as I praise God! Fill me up Jesus! I fully expect to receive my prayer language as You give me utterance. In Jesus' Name. Amen.

Now, out loud, begin to praise and glorify JESUS, because He is the baptizer of the Holy Spirit! From deep in your spirit, tell Him, "I love you, I thank you, I praise you, Jesus."

Repeat this as you feel joy and gratefulness bubble up from deep inside you. Speak those words and syllables you receive – not in your own language, but the heavenly language given to you by the Holy Spirit. Allow this joy to come out of you in syllables of a language your own mind does not already know. That will be your prayer language the Spirit will use through you when you don't know how to pray (Romans 8:26-28). It is not the "gift of tongues" for public use, therefore it does not require a public interpretation.

You have to surrender and use your own vocal chords to verbally express your new prayer language. The Holy Spirit is a gentleman. He will not force you to speak. Don't be concerned with how it sounds. It is a heavenly language!

Worship Him! Praise Him! Use your heavenly language by praying in the Spirit every day! Paul urges us to *"pray in the Spirit on all occasions with all kinds of prayers and requests."* (Ephesians 6:18)

Notes

Notes

Notes

Notes

Notes

Notes

Notes

Notes

Notes

Book of Remembrance

Rescue, Redemption, and Relationship

ALL BOOKS AVAILABLE AT WWW.FIJM.ORG

Devotion and Discipleship

After being on top of the world with a CPA office on Park Avenue, Stephen Canup lost it all and found himself homeless and incarcerated. ***Jail-House Religion*** is his true life story on God's redeeming love and grace.

Stephen's second book, ***Diving Deeper***, is a daily discipleship field guide that encourages and challenges the reader into a more abundant life of freedom and renewal.

Ex-convicts and felons in general, and former sex offenders in particular, are treated as modern day lepers. ***Lepers No More*** illustrates how society's outcasts are healed and restored.

Knowing God Series

Thinking about establishing a relationship with God can be intimidating. However, seeking and maintaining one with each of the three persons of the Godhead is achievable—Father, Son, and Holy Spirit! Learn how in this series.

These books are available at the Freedom in Jesus website www.fijm.org for friends and family to purchase for themselves or for someone they love. (Shipping into a correctional facility is available.)

Preview books at www.stephencanup.com

IN JESUS
PRISON MINISTRIES

STEPHEN CANUP

AND

FREEDOM IN JESUS PRISON MINISTRIES

HEARTILY RECOMMENDS

KINGDOM TOWERS

LUBBOCK, TX

AS A GREAT PLACE TO START OVER!

MAKING RE-ENTRY A
COMPLETE SUCCESS
WITH A SUPPORTIVE LIVING ENVIRONMENT

KINGDOM TOWERS
LOVE. SERVE. RESTORE.

Kingdom Towers offers a residential transition program operated under and emphasizing Christian principles.

Our approach is to offer a safe and sober environment in which men can learn to love, serve, and commit to restoring their lives and relationships.

"You will have complete support from staff and residents."
~ J.B. Cline

"God put me in this place to be a servant."
~ B. Lee

FOR DETAILS & AN APPLICATION PLEASE CALL OR WRITE
1629 16th St, Lubbock, Texas 79401 | (806)777-6213 | ktlubbocktx.com

After his salvation in prison in 2009, Stephen Canup's study of God's Word awakened his desire to encourage and teach others. As a result, it became natural to write down quotations, and short paragraphs that inspire, teach and encourage. Certainly, these "keepsakes" are part of the spiritual warfare weapons arsenal that God has provided Stephen to help equip others.

Over the years, his "go to" place to record the wisdom gems he found in his studies is in the back of his favorite Bibles. He shares them here in this book in the hope they will bless you as they have blessed him.

**THE OLD STEPHEN
BEFORE PRISON
2008**

**THE NEW STEPHEN
AFTER PRISON
2012**

Stephen Canup is the President of Freedom in Jesus Prison Ministries and the author of the book *Jail-House Religion: From Park Avenue... to Park Bench... to Prison*, which has over 350,000 copies in print. All seven of his books are available for preview at *www.stephencanup.com*

Freedom
IN JESUS
PRISON MINISTRIES

P.O. Box 939 • Levelland, TX 79336
info@fijm.org • www.fijm.org

$15.00
ISBN 978-1-7352529-8-8

www.ingramcontent.com/pod-product-compliance
Lightning Source LLC
Chambersburg PA
CBHW072156070526
44585CB00015B/1172